# Making Good Men Better

*A 52 Week Personal Growth Plan*
*Based on the Teachings of Freemasonry*

Carl W. Davis

# Acknowledgments

This book is dedicated to the man who first introduced me to Freemasonry, my childhood pastor and Masonic Brother, the Reverend William J. Jones, and to who all who seek more light.

Masons learn from one another. I have spent years visiting lodges all over the United States and making a study of the different rituals that are used around the world. It would be impossible to list the name of every Freemason who has taught me life lessons, Masonic ideas or historical information about our Craft. I am deeply indebted to each person who has taken time to help make me a better person by their example, helpful words, listening ears, supporting presence and brotherly love.

I specifically wish to thank my friend and Masonic Brother Ted Jackson who has served as editor of this book as well as an editor of my first book <u>Because Donors Want to Share: A Donor- Centric Approach to Individual Fundraising</u>. Ted's powerful command of language, his patience with me throughout the writing process, and most importantly, his personal friendship and love, mean more to me than I can articulate.

While the work of an editor is invaluable, and ideas come from many places, any mistakes or errors in this work are completely my own.

# About the Author

Carl W. Davis was Initiated as an Entered Apprentice, Passed to the Degree of Fellowcraft and Raised to the Sublime Degree of Master Mason in Peru-Miami Lodge #67 F&AM in Peru, Indiana. He served as Master of that lodge in 2005. In 2008 he moved to Chicago, Illinois where he joined Hesperia Lodge #411 AF&AM. In 2015 he relocated to North Carolina where he joined The Lodge of the Nine Sisters #773 AF&AM in Raleigh, North Carolina. He is also an honorary member of Naphtali Lodge #389 in Center, Indiana, and a 32nd Degree member of the Ancient Accepted Scottish Rite Valley of Indianapolis.

He can be reached by writing to Blunderbuss Books Post Office Box 57281 New Orleans, Louisiana 70157

Making Good Men Better: _A 52 Week Personal Growth Plan Based on the Teachings of Freemasonry_
Author: Carl W. Davis, Past Master
Editor: Theodore S. Jackson, PhD
Publisher: Blunderbuss Books
Post Office Box 57281 New Orleans, Louisiana 70157
ISBN: 978-0-578-63356-5

# Introduction

There is no single voice that speaks for all of Freemasonry. By organizational design each Grand Lodge is sovereign in its own affairs. In practice each individual Freemason applies the teachings of our Craft to his own life in his own way at his own time.

This reality is itself a teaching of Freemasonry. We often describe it in our ritual language as the value of tolerance. It is also known as pluralism. Each of us is free to look at a symbol, find a life enriching interpretation of that symbol, and then apply that lesson to our life as we see fit. Another Mason may look at the same symbol that I examine in this book and find a totally different meaning and then apply that meaning to his life in a way that is totally different from the way I do. Both applications can be valid at the same time. At the Grand Lodge level, one Grand Lodge may offer a section of degree ritual for its members that uses specific language while a different Grand Lodge will offer a different section of ritual with different words for the same degree. All are good and the experience of one does not negate the experience of the other.

Masonry teaches us that it is okay, even good, to have different understandings of concepts than our brothers. Just because one interpretation is right for one person does not mean that a different interpretation is wrong for another person who sees it differently. Both understandings can co-exist with equal validity and both brothers can benefit from considering the understanding and perspective of the other. Consider the Masonic significance of the Letter G. It reminds us of more than one thing when we see it.

As you read this book you will be exposed to my opinions about how certain Masonic symbols and teachings can apply to our lives. You may think of other applications of these symbols as well. You are encouraged to write your ideas and thoughts in the notes section of each chapter. My ideas are in no way offered as the only way to apply Freemasonry's teachings. They are merely a way to apply them to your life that you may find helpful. This book is not published by any Grand Lodge or Masonic authority. It is based on no individual ritual tradition. As you read this book you may encounter phrases that are familiar to you and you may be exposed to phrases that are new I have made a study of Masonic ritual from several Grand Jurisdictions and have been informed by both York and Scottish Rite Craft Lodge traditions from several jurisdictions in the United States and Canada. This book focuses on symbols, lessons and values that are common across Freemasonry and draws upon many different ritual traditions to communicate them.

This book is devotional, not academic in nature. I will therefore leave the history of the different ritual traditions to the scholars and focus only on the application of Freemasonry's moral teachings. Each Mason who reads this book is encouraged to consider, study and reflect upon the specific ritual teachings of his own Lodge's ritual.

I believe that this book's greatest contribution will not be the specific ideas it offers but rather the opportunity it presents for any person to regularly and systematically put the teachings of Freemasonry into their daily life.

The book consists of 52 chapters. I designed it to be read one chapter per week over the course of a year. After each chapter is a page designed for you to write your own thoughts and ideas about that week's topic. I hope that by regularly reflecting on the teachings of Freemasonry in this intentional way each reader will find that he is a good man made better.

Carl W. Davis, PM
North Carolina
Summer 2019

Note: Italicized words in the text of this book are from Masonic ritual.

# Table of Contents

# Nobler Deeds, Higher Thoughts, Greater Achievements

Freemasons believe that we should always try to do better. While celebrating our success today we also want to do even greater things tomorrow. We are never complacent with our work, nor do we ever think that our current standard is as good as it can get. We are always seeking to improve. We respectfully look at the splendid accomplishments of those who have gone before us with gratitude for their labor and respect for their impact. While we do that, we are also doing our level best to continue the upward trajectory of their work through our own efforts now. All the while we are dreaming of how the next generation will reach even higher heights than we can obtain today. In this great work of advancement, growth, and progress, the whole human race is linked; generation to generation, in an upward trajectory planned by the Great Architect of the Universe himself. We must strive to be better all the time.

A phrase that is often used to describe Freemasonry is "Making Good Men Better." The truth is that the structure of Freemasonry does very little to accomplish that goal itself. Instead, the ritualized teachings of Freemasonry are made available to every Freemason as he is initiated as an Entered Apprentice, passed to the degree of Fellowcraft, and raised to the sublime degree of Master Mason. Once he learns the teachings of our ritual, it is up to each individual Freemason to apply those teachings to his life. It is in the application of those teachings that he becomes better.

In this way each Freemason strives towards Nobler Deeds, Higher Thoughts, and Greater Achievements in his personal life through daily growth, even as the human race does from generation to generation.

_____

_____

_____

_____

_____

_____

_____

_____

_____

_____

_____

_____

_____

_____

_____

_____

_____

_____

_____

_____

# 24 Inch Gauge

Some people are very productive and others get nothing done.

This is not because some people have more time than others do since every person on earth gets the same amount of time per day. In this way we are all equal.

It is occasionally suggested that one way to solve all of society's problems might be to ensure that each person has the same amount of money. Maybe if we each had the same resources we could all reach the same level of success. This idea is proven false by the fact that each person does get the same amount of time each day and yet some use that time for great progress and others do nothing constructive at all over the same period of 24 hours. The power to make progress does not so much depend on how much we have, but on how well we use what we do have.

Time is the most precious resource there is because all the money in the world cannot buy one extra minute of it.

The difference between the people who do great things and the people who do little to contribute to the betterment of humankind is not in how much time they have each day but instead is found in how they use their time. Therefore, time management is one of the most important skills we can have and that's why time management is addressed with the very first working tool in Masonry, The 24 Inch Gauge. One of the first lessons a new Freemason is taught is how to rightly divide his time.

We are taught that the management of our time should be guided by three equally important principles. Namely, the worship and service of God, productively improving society through our chosen vocational service, and time for rest and refreshment.

Freemasonry teaches that we are all children of God who created us in His image. Because of that reality, our chief duty is to worship and revere God who is our Father and our Maker. The word worship means to ascribe worth. When an inventor creates a new product or an engineer designs a new machine, the best way that creation can ascribe worth to its creator is to function as it was designed and built. Sitting in my living room is a 100-year-old typewriter. The fact that it still works and can be used now is a great credit to the people who designed and built it more than a century ago. So it should be with us towards God. We were created to know and love both God and our fellow man. When we live lives transformed by our knowledge of God's love for us so much that we naturally love the other people in our lives, then we ascribe worth to our Creator by functioning as we were designed to function.

This takes us to the second way we should use our time, in ways that make our world better. We do this when we make moral choices in our personal and professional lives. When we treat others as we would like to be treated, when we do the right thing even if we don't think anyone is looking. We make the world better when we give every task we perform our level best. We make the world better when we take good care of the things we are responsible for. In these ways, and in others, we rightly divide our time.

Many people consider rest to be a waste of time. When a person is asked "What did you do last weekend?" He may reply "Oh, nothing, I just rested." Such a view that rest is nothing, or less important than other ways that our time should be used is wrong. In the Genesis creation story that is known to all Masons from our ritual, God commands His creation to both work and to rest with equal importance. We are designed to rest. Therefore, our rest is as much a worship of God as our work is.

Failure to rest appropriately is as much a misuse of our time as failure to work appropriately is. Rest can take many forms and we need both physical, mental and emotional rest in order to function at our best, as we were designed. Never be ashamed to use your time for rest and relaxation.

Consider making a list of everything you plan to do today and color code it based on which of those three categories the task falls into. Prayer, Bible study, devotional reading, volunteering, and helping others can fall into the first category. All tasks related to your employment fall into the second category.

Tasks that refresh your body and spirit fall into the third category. This would include sleep, exercise, and hobby related activities.

Are each of the three categories equally represented? Who else do you involve in these activities? Which ones do you do with your spouse, children, family and friends, and which ones do you do alone? Are you happy with that balance or is there a place where you can make an adjustment to become better at rightly dividing your time?

_____

_____

_____

_____

_____

_____

_____

_____

_____

_____

_____

_____

_____

_____

_____

_____

_____

# A Claim Upon Your Kind Offices

Masons believe that we have an obligation to help others. In helping others, we perform the duty that our Creator created us to perform and therefore in the performance of this duty we find fulfillment and satisfaction.

Every Mason will do all he can to help a brother Mason to the extent that he is able to be of assistance to a worthy brother in need. Our obligation to help others extends even beyond that sacred commitment that all Masons make.

In the Christian Scriptures, Jesus tells a story which has come to be known as the "Parable of the Good Samaritan." The story is recorded in the tenth chapter of the Gospel According to Saint Luke as follows:

"[25] And, behold, a certain lawyer stood up, and tempted him [Jesus], saying, Master, what shall I do to inherit eternal life? [26] He said unto him, What is written in the law? how readest thou? [27] And he answering said, Thou shalt love the Lord thy God with all thy heart, and with all thy soul, and with all thy strength, and with all thy mind; and thy neighbour as thyself. [28] And he said unto him, Thou hast answered right: this do, and thou shalt live. [29] But he, willing to justify himself, said unto Jesus, And who is my neighbour? [30] And Jesus answering said, A certain *man* went down from Jerusalem to Jericho, and fell among thieves, which stripped him of his raiment, and wounded *him*, and departed, leaving *him* half dead. [31] And by chance there came down a certain priest that way: and when he saw him, he passed by on the other side. [32] And likewise a Levite, when he was at the place, came and looked *on him*, and passed by on the other side. [33] But a certain Samaritan, as he journeyed, came where he was: and when he saw him, he had compassion *on him*, [34] And went to *him*, and bound up his wounds, pouring in oil and wine, and set him on his own beast, and brought him to an inn, and took care of him. [35] And on the morrow when he departed, he took out two pence, and gave *them* to the host, and said unto him, Take care of him; and whatsoever thou spendest more, when I come again, I will repay thee. [36] Which now of these three, thinkest thou, was neighbour unto him that fell among the thieves? [37] And he said, He that shewed mercy on him. Then said Jesus unto him, Go, and do thou likewise"

In some Masonic ritual traditions Masons end their lodge meeting by specifically reflecting on the opportunities that we as

Freemasons have to help one another in our daily lives. Then the charge is given "*And these generous principles are to extend further; every human being has a claim upon your kind offices; wherefore we enjoin it upon you: do good unto all.*"

Who is your neighbor? How can you best do good unto all using the time, treasure and talent that God has given to you this week?

_____

_____

_____

_____

_____

_____

_____

_____

_____

_____

_____

_____

_____

_____

_____

_____

_____

_____

# A Set of Winding Stairs

In many ritual traditions, being passed to the second degree of Masonry requires the candidate to ascend a flight of winding stairs consisting of three, five, and seven steps.

This teaches the value of education and reminds us that education is a never-ending, life- long process. On each of the first three steps the new Fellowcraft is taught specific facts and pieces of interesting historical information. Then, as the staircase turns and he climbs the next five steps he learns even more about concepts and theories. It can feel overwhelming, but the journey continues and with the next turn he is faced with seven more steps. Each of those steps is marked by even deeper learning and an exposure to worlds of new knowledge. Then, finally when the stair case is fully ascended, he comes not to an end, but to a door that opens to an entirely new world of opportunities for learning and growth. He could not have reached that door unless he had painstakingly taken each of the steps that led to it, one at a time. Each step was a prerequisite for the next and prepared the traveler for what awaited him in his future.

So it is in life. We begin learning in the earliest years of our childhood and the process does not end until our time on earth is complete. The lessons of yesterday have prepared us for today: what we do and learn today can be used to help us do even better tomorrow. We must pay attention and learn the lessons of life and not simply rush from one task to the next without taking time to learn from our past and present.

During his ascent up the staircase the Fellowcraft is guided by a wise friend who has already traveled the path. This is to teach us that in life, we must be willing to accept the instruction and wisdom of others who are with us on our journey and we must be willing to assist those who are traveling with us.

# The Bee Hive

In many jurisdictions Masons are taught *that it could have pleased God to make man independent of all other beings, but as dependence is one of the strongest bonds of society, mankind was made dependent on each other for protection and security, as they thereby enjoy better opportunities for fulfilling the duties of reciprocal love and friendship.*

Many people in our society falsely believe that each person should be totally independent. The truth is that this is not how the Great Architect of the Universe chose to design us. God chose to make us interdependent not independent. This is why it is so good and pleasant for brothers to dwell together in unity. In so doing, we honor God by functioning according to our design.

No individual person has every skill that is needed in a community. No person is able to meet every challenge or accomplish every goal alone. Also, every one of us has something of value to contribute. The lesson of this symbol is that each of us must use our strengths and abilities together with the different, yet equally vital, strengths and abilities of others in order to meet the needs of society in an intentional, respectful, and organized fashion.

We must always be ready to offer or help to others as well as receive the help of others. The interdependent nature of humanity requires each of us to both give and receive assistance. It is in this giving and receiving that our friendships are strengthened and God who created us to function this way is worshiped.

Masonry has chosen the emblem of the bee hive to teach this important truth because individually each bee is small and unable to accomplish everything that must be done. Yet, because bees organize themselves with such great efficiency and cohesion they are able to function together as a great force with high productivity and little waste. So may it be with us as we work together to make ourselves and our world better.

_____

_____

_____

_____

_____

_____

_____

_____

_____

_____

_____

_____

_____

_____

_____

_____

_____

# Brotherly Love, Relief, and Truth

Have you heard the story of the young boy whose family moved to a new town where he had to go to a new school? The other children in the new school were not welcoming of him. They would not talk to him at the bus stop, they never invited him to join any of their teams or to attend their birthday parties. No one ever came over to invite the boy to play outside. Yet he was never discouraged. It appeared to his mother that he was unaware that he was unpopular. She fretted over him a great deal when Valentine's Day approached. Her son was very excited about the day and looked forward to participating in the school's tradition of making heart-shaped cards out of construction paper and giving them to one's friends during school on February 14th. Every day after school for a week before Valentine's Day the boy worked hard making very beautiful cards for every child in his class, and everyone who rode the same bus as him to and from school each day. His mother watched and worried about how disappointed he would be when he came home from school on Valentine's day having given out so many Valentines yet, she feared, receiving very few in return.

After a week of preparation the day finally arrived and he went off to school with his book bag overflowing with the red paper hearts trimmed in white paper lace for all of his classmates. He beamed with excitement and brimmed with energy as he looked forward to the day at school. His mother tried to hide her anxiety that morning as she sent him off.

When the bus came that afternoon, the mother was watching out of the window, waiting to see her son, imagining that he would be downcast and sad. To her surprise he was full of joy and energy as he bounded off of the bus and skipped to their home. His mother welcomed him home and asked him how his day had been. "Wonderful!" he replied. "I gave Valentines to everyone on the bus and everyone in my class!"

His mother noticed that he didn't seem to have any Valentines in his book bag and so she asked him "How many of your classmates gave you a card?" "Oh, none" he said, undaunted. His mother was puzzled and asked "Then, why are you so happy, son?" He replied, "Because now they all know that I love them!"

Freemasons are called to exhibit the beauties of Brotherly Love, Relief and Truth. It is easy to love others who clearly love us in return. It is easy to relieve the suffering of those who are visibly appreciative and it is easy to proclaim the truth where it is instantly welcomed. But our work does not end there. We must also be a beacon of Brotherly Love even to those who reject its warm, welcoming embrace. We must relieve the distressed even when they do not say thank you and we must proclaim the truth of the universal brotherhood of man under the universal parenthood of God, even when such a notion is rejected by the culture in which we live.

A radio beacon continually transmits its message even if no one is listening at that moment. A lighthouse continually shines its light even if there is no one looking for a while. So it must be with us. We must continually love others even when they reject that love or cannot bring themselves to accept our earnest expression of it. Our job is not to have our love accepted but to live it into existence through the way we treat and communicate with others regardless of their reactions. Like the boy in the story of the Valentines, we have done our duty when people know they are loved, even if they do not give us that love in return.

We must relieve the distressed even when they are unappreciative of our assistance. This duty is incumbent upon all Freemasons and someday we will hear the words *Well done thou good and faithful servant* even if we do not hear the words "thank you" now.

We live in a world where some people seem to be of greater worth than others and where many people believe they are not worthy of love and acceptance because it is what they have been taught their whole lives. Freemasonry proclaims the truth that everyone of us is a child of God, the Grand Architect of the whole universe, not just of a specific group or culture. As we proclaim this notion we will likely be dismissed by many as being unsophisticated for our belief in the universal fatherhood of God and the corresponding brotherhood of man. Yet, the truth remains true and we remain committed to spreading that truth.

_____

_____

_____

_____

_____

_____

_____

_____

_____

_____

_____

_____

_____

_____

_____

_____

_____

_____

# Chalk, Charcoal, and Clay

Masonic ritual makes use of chalk, charcoal, and clay to teach three of our core values. Namely; freedom, fervency, and zeal.

Freemasonry values freedom greatly. It is for this reason that tyrants have always persecuted Freemasons and many great liberators of society have been members of our gentle craft. The name of our order begins with the word "free" because, as our tradition tells us, even in the ancient days of European serfdom, Masons were allowed to travel and work freely according to their own desires and discretion. Their skills were in such demand that no prince or ruler could contain them. For this reason, ancient Masons guarded their trade secrets diligently because it was that information about how to build great buildings from stone that ensured their continual freedom.

Today Freemasons also guard freedom from anyone who would attempt to destroy it. Within our own Craft, each brother is free to interpret and apply the teachings of our ritual to his own life according to the dictates of his own conscience and understanding. This idea is *represented by chalk because chalk is so freely formed that even at the slightest touch it gives way.*

Freemasons are fervent in our work to make ourselves better men. We begin this journey in youth and continue it through manhood and old age, never ending our journey of self- improvement until it pleases God to end our time on this earth. This fervency is represented by charcoal *because when charcoal is burned it creates a heat so fervent that even metal can be bent and formed.*

Freemasons have great zeal. Zeal is great energy or enthusiasm in pursuit of a cause. This energy is what motivates us to continue or life-long work and never become discouraged even when we are going through difficult times. Zeal makes our work practical and effective and is represented by *clay because clay is a very practical material that can be used for making many different things.*

# Charity

In 1772 Masonic philosopher William Preston wrote, "To relieve the distressed is a duty incumbent on all men, but particularly on Freemasons, who are linked together by an indissoluble chain of sincere affection. To soothe the unhappy, to sympathize with their misfortunes, to compassionate their miseries, and to restore peace to their troubled minds, is the great aim we have in view. On this basis we form our friendships and establish our connections."

In the Christian tradition, Jesus says in Luke 12:48 "to whom much is given, much will be required." This idea is a moral adage that transcends religious differences. While articulated clearly in the Christian scriptures, the idea is not exclusive to Christianity.

Freemasons of all religions understand that we have an obligation to help people who are suffering. As Freemasons, we know the love of caring brothers and the security of being connected to other men who share our values and who consider our welfare and happiness equal with that of their own. We can travel to any corner of the world and meet a brother in whose fidelity we can safely confide. This privileged position comes with a corresponding duty to do what we can to assist those who are not so blessed.

Thomas S. Monson said "Charity is having patience with someone who has let us down. It is resisting the impulse to become offended easily. It is accepting weakness and shortcomings. It is accepting people as they truly are. It is looking beyond physical appearances to attributes that will not dim through time. It is resisting the impulse to categorize others."

It is this motivation that has caused Freemasons to build orphanages, homes for the aged, schools, to provide funding for education, and to give medical care for those in need.

But moving beyond those obvious examples of Masonic Charity, let us consider how we can be friends to the lonely, listeners to those whose voices are not being heard, and helpers to those struggling with things that only the observant can see.

# Checkered Floor

The floor of a Masonic Lodge is made up of a black and white tiled floor in a checkerboard pattern. As a person walks across the lodge room he will step upon an equal number of black and white tiles. In fact, one foot may be on a black tile while the other foot is on a white tile!

So it is as we travel through life. We will go through some good times and some hard times. Knowing that life is full of both we should never feel too discouraged during the hard days nor should we feel too proud during the easy times. We must also know that life, being full of both, will never be all joy nor all sorrow, but will always be a combination of experiences.

Every member of the lodge moves across the same floor from the Worshipful Master to the lowest Entered Apprentice. So it is in life. The greatest, wealthiest and most respected members of our society move through their ups and downs as do the lowest and least regarded members of our community. This experience is universal throughout all of humanity. It is a false idea to think "If I just had a better job, or more money (or anything else) then my life would be easy." It is also foolish to think "If I didn't have (a particular trait, talent or possession) then I would have no joy in my life." All of us travel through life over a checkerboard floor.

We must therefore be sensitive to the reality that others are also passing through life with the same mixture of happiness and sorrow in their lives. We should therefore be sensitive to their needs as we hope they are sensitive towards ours. When we are in a bright spot we must be conscious and courteous of those who are in dark places. When we are in a dark place we must not let that dim the brightness that our brother may be experiencing in his life at that same moment.

Mourn with those who mourn and rejoice with those who rejoice, knowing that all of our lives will include both.

# The Chisel

The Chisel is a working tool that is not used in every ritual tradition but is a tool that every Freemason will find useful.

An operative Mason uses the chisel to remove flaws from a stone or gem to show its inner beauty. We as Speculative Masons use the chisel to remind us of the importance of discipline and education in our life. Masonic ritual teaches that "Just as the brilliance of the diamond is revealed by the skillful use of the chisel, so too will the beauties of the human mind be revealed through knowledge."

Freemasons value education and knowledge. We must each strive to gain as much knowledge as possible and encourage others to do the same.

Education and knowledge come to us through the formal classroom opportunities provided at colleges and universities. It is the belief in the value of this education that motivates many Masonic Lodges to offer scholarships to the young people of their community.

As Freemasons, we remember that education and knowledge can be gained in other ways too. In ancient days an apprentice was taught by a master. We use this model of learning in all three of our masonic degrees today, thus illustrating the message that each of us can learn from those who are laboring with us and have been on the job of life longer than us. It also teaches us that as we have been taught, so we must be willing to teach those who come behind us.

A true Freemason wishes to reach his personal educational potential and help others to reach theirs, too.

# Compass

The primary symbol used to represent Freemasonry is the Square and Compass. In some places the tool is called the "compass" and in other jurisdictions it is referred to as the "compasses." This is the same tool, just referred to by different names in different ritual traditions.

Stone masons use compasses to draw circles. They can also be used to draft, measure distance, and even navigate using maps and charts. The lesson of the compass lies within its two moveable legs. As the compass can only open so wide, so there are boundaries to everything. Some rituals tell us that *The Compasses, in defining limits and proportions, teach us the limits of good and evil as laid down by the Great Architect.*

We must know the limit of our own capabilities and not attempt to do things that are beyond our limits. We must also accept the limits that other people have. We must not be afraid or ashamed to communicate our limits with others and we must graciously accept when others inform us of their limitations.

Only when we accurately understand our own limits and the limits of others can we truly work together to achieve our shared goals.

This tool teaches us to use proportion and balance in our work and life. Doing so brings about stability and beauty in both.

_____

_____

_____

_____

_____

_____

_____

_____

_____

_____

_____

_____

_____

_____

_____

_____

_____

_____

_____

## Consider a Brother's Welfare and Happiness Equal with That of Your Own

Jealousy is one of the greatest enemies of happiness. That is one reason Masons are taught to always consider our brother's welfare and happiness equal with that of our own. When we truly love another person we desire nothing but the best for that person. When another person has great success, we feel that joy as much as if it had happened to us personally. When a brother has a great sorrow, we feel the pain as if it was ours as well. That is how Masons are to feel about others and why we are charged to "Consider a brother's welfare and happiness equal with that of our own."

Just as being jealous of another person can destroy one's happiness, being happy for another person can increase one's level of personal joy. The next time you hear that a friend has gotten a promotion, a new possession or had a positive change in his life, celebrate his success as if it were your own.

Similarly, if you have the opportunity to help a brother make a positive change in his life, work towards making that happen as hard as you would work as if you were working to make that positive change happen for yourself.

Considering the welfare and happiness of another person is the natural result of truly loving them. Years ago I was living on the second floor of a three story apartment building in Chicago. It seemed to me that my upstairs neighbors must have worn iron shoes and liked to tap dance 24 hours a day. I was constantly annoyed by the sound of footsteps above me. I was very happy the day those neighbors moved out. Then an unexpected thing happened. An old friend of mine from Detroit moved to Chicago and just happened to rent the apartment right above me. Honestly, my friend Matt was no quieter than the previous neighbors. But I was no longer bothered by the noise because now when I heard the footsteps I thought of Matt and how happy I was to be living so close to him after such a long absence. My love for Matt easily overcame my annoyance at the sound of footsteps from upstairs because now the noises I heard were not just annoyances to my routine made by some faceless stranger as they had been before, now they were the sounds of my friend.

Let brotherly love prevail and let us consider our brother's welfare and happiness equally with that of our own as every moral and social virtue cement us.

# First Invoking the Blessing of Deity

Freemasons are taught that we should invoke the blessing of Deity before any great or important undertaking. While this basic idea may seem obvious for any group which only admits people into its membership who profess a belief in God, it is a very important lesson to remember. How many of us have only thought to turn to prayer after our plans have started to run into trouble?

James Montgomery famously said "prayer is the soul's sincere desire, uttered or unexpressed." Freemasonry teaches that God is the Father of all humanity and all of us are encouraged to communicate with him through prayer in the ways that feel best to us. Each Freemason is encouraged to find his own path to God according to his own faith tradition and understanding. There are good Freemasons of almost every religion imaginable. One thing they each hold in common is that they pray.

Follow the example of one illustrious in Masonic history, King Solomon, who tradition tells us, was the wisest man to ever live. When he needed guidance, he turned to God in prayer and he found a solution to the problem he faced.

*Thou, O God, knowest our down-sitting and our uprising, and understandest our thoughts afar off. Shield and defend us from the evil intentions of our enemies, and support us under the trials and afflictions we are destined to endure while traveling through this vale of tears. Man that is born of a woman is of few days and full of trouble. He cometh forth as a flower and is cut down; he fleeth also as a shadow, and continueth not. Seeing his days are determined, the number of his months are with Thee; Thou hast appointed his bounds that he cannot pass; turn from him that he may rest till he shall accomplish his day.*

*For there is hope of a tree, if it be cut down, that it will sprout again, and that the tender branch thereof will not cease. But man dieth and wasteth away; yea, man giveth up the ghost, and where is he? As the waters fail from the sea, and the flood decayeth and drieth up, so man lieth down and riseth not up till the heavens shall be no more. Yet, O Lord! have compassion on the children of Thy creation; administer them comfort in time of trouble, and save them with an everlasting salvation! Amen.*

A Freemason is a man of prayer.

# Fortitude

Masonic ritual teaches that *fortitude is that noble and steady purpose of mind, whereby we are enabled to undergo any pain, peril, or danger, when prudentially deemed expedient. This virtue is equally distant from rashness and cowardice; and, like the former, should be deeply impressed upon the mind of every Mason, as a safeguard against any illegal attack that may be made, by force or otherwise, to extort from him any of those valuable secrets with which he has been so solemnly entrusted, and which were emblematically represented upon his first admission into the Lodge.*

Steadfast bravery is another way to describe fortitude. For the Mason, fortitude symbolizes more than mere physical strength and courage. Fortitude means moral courage.

A man I greatly respect and work with in my professional capacity came to this country from India as a young man. He is now in his 70s and has been very successful in just about every way that success can be measured. He told me that one key to his success was that he has always been willing to do the thing that no one else was doing. When others found a job too hard or too disagreeable, Mark engaged the opportunity with fortitude.

Like our fabled Grand Master Hiram Abiff, we Freemasons must have the strength and ability to make a decision based upon our own moral convictions and stick to it regardless of the consequences.

As Freemasons we work to exhibit the highest moral and ethical principles in our lifestyles and stand by those principles even if society may look unfavorably upon them.

# Give Good and Timely Counsel, in the Most Tender Way

Freemasons are bound to each other by sacred commitments to always value the other's welfare and happiness equal with that of our own. We share the same moral values of continual self-improvement and a desire to always behave honorably, justly, fairly, mercifully, and kindly. We are committed to helping each other in our efforts to be good men in the daily living of our lives.

With the relationship that Freemasons have with each other comes the opportunity to both give and receive counsel. When we see a brother who is traveling down a path that we ourselves have taken in the past we can help him by telling him what we wish we had known when we were in his place. Similarly, when we find ourselves in a quandary we have a world of brothers who we can ask for advice and guidance as well.

The Freemason does not offer his counsel in a condescending or holier than thou tone. He does not offer it publically where embarrassment might result. He does not offer it out of a feeling of superiority or from a place of judgement. Instead, he offers it gently and lovingly so that the brother receiving it feels loved and supported along his journey of life.

The counsel should not come in the form you "you must do this. . ." Instead it should be founded upon the guiding brother's personal experiences of "for me, in my life, I have found that. . ." It must always be motivated by a loving concern for the other brother and rooted on the bedrock principle that the loving brotherly relationship will not be negatively impacted even if the brother chooses not to heed the counsel given. Each Freemason is free to make his own choices and our efforts are merely to provide him with the best counsel possible for use in his decision making process. Our relationships are not based on our advice being followed, but rather on the realty that we are brothers, bound by a sacred covenant which cannot be broken.

In this environment, Freemasons are free to be vulnerable with one another and both seek and give wise counsel in the most tender of ways.

# Harmony Being the Strength and Support of All Societies, More Especially of Ours

In music, harmony does not mean that many different instruments play the same note at the same time. Instead, it means that many different notes are played at the same time, and as the sounds all come together in the ear of the listener, the resulting sound is something even more pleasant and powerful than simply listening to any individual note would be.

It is the same with Freemasons. We are not all identical. We do not all think the same. We do not share the same personal or professional goals. We are each unique and each one of us is respected by every other Freemason for our unique identity. When we live our unique lives together as brothers in this world we create a more pleasant and powerful impact than we could if we simply carried on alone. We can do more together than any of us could do alone.

Many of us have been taught in our Lodge the value of the words recorded in Ecclesiastes 4:10-12 whose author is reported to be King Solomon; "Two *are* better than one; because they have a good reward for their labour. For if they fall, the one will lift up his fellow: but woe to him *that is* alone when he falleth; for *he hath* not another to help him up. Again, if two lie together, then they have heat: but how can one be warm *alone*? And if one prevail against him, two shall withstand him; and a threefold cord is not quickly broken." This scripture is read in some Masonic Jurisdictions as part of their ritual.

No Freemason is ever alone. He always has the support of his brothers, even the ones he has yet to meet; *harmony, being the strength and support of all societies, more especially of ours.*

# Honor

The figure who plays the greatest role in Masonic ritual is King Solomon who is credited with writing the following words in the 22$^{nd}$ chapter of Proverbs. "A *good* name *is* rather to be chosen than great riches, *and* loving favour rather than silver and gold. The rich and poor meet together: the LORD *is* the maker of them all."

These words from the wisest man who ever lived remind us of the importance of honor. It is better to be well regarded than it is to be rich. And, honor is a virtue that both rich and poor men may possess because every person is equally made in the image of God. Honor is a virtue that must define every true Freemason.

Synonyms for honor are: integrity, uprightness, high principles, righteousness, rectitude, nobility, high- mindedness, right-mindedness, and noble-mindedness. Honor has to do with our state of mind because our state of mind governs our thoughts and our actions. Masons are charged to walk uprightly in our several stations before God and man.

In the course of any given day we will have many opportunities to take action and in each of those cases we may choose to do something that is either honorable or less than honorable. As men of honor, we will make choices that are right in our dealings with others even when making such a choice may not benefit us as much materially as making a different choice. I am reminded of a Mason I know who owns a company in an industry where workers are paid notoriously low wages. This brother chooses to pay his employees more than his competitors pay their employees because he believes it to be the right and honorable decision to pay his workers enough money that they can afford to live on their salaries. That choice may result in our brother's company being less profitable, but that choice also results in his employees holding him in high esteem. Our Brother truly understands the message of our most excellent Grand Master King Solomon "A *good* name *is* rather to be chosen than great riches, *and* loving favour rather than silver and gold."

# Hoodwink

The best tasting meals come when we are the most hungry. The most appreciated rest comes after a day of very hard work and the most satisfying drink of water comes when we are the most parched.

Likewise, to truly appreciate light a person must first experience darkness. This is a lesson of the hoodwink or blindfold as used in the rituals of Freemasonry.

We also act upon truth taught by this symbol when we realize that each day offers us the opportunity to learn and apply new ideas in our lives. Today we may see things that we were blind to only yesterday. If we approach life with an open mind then we never stop seeing the light of new opportunities and brighter prospects.

Yet, if we refuse to see the progress that comes from challenging our old understandings when we observe new data, then we will continue to be blind to the blessings that surround us.

It is up to each of us to remove the hoodwink of our own prejudices, assumptions, stubbornness, complacency and laziness each day and grow in the light that surrounds us.

# Jachin and Boaz

In many Masonic Lodges there stand two pillars. These represent the two pillars that were reported to stand in King Solomon's Temple. One is named Jachin and the other Boaz. Together they remind us of strength and establishment.

Strength is required in our work to make ourselves better. We must be strong as we seek to treat others fairly and with kindness in all of our daily actions as it is not always easy to make such decisions. We must be strong in keeping our commitments to be honest and authentic in all of our relationships and to help others to the best of our ability when we see them in need and have the ability to assist.

We must be strong to keep our commitment to pray for others even as we pray for ourselves.

Establishment comes as a result of strength over time. The longer that we are strong, the more established we become. Over many years of intentional efforts at moral and honest living we establish ourselves as moral leaders in our families and communities. We establish a tradition of doing the right thing that both improves our own lives as well as the lives of those around us.

The Freemason is reminded of these truths when he sees the twin pillars of Jachin and Boaz in his lodge room.

What commitments have you made and kept lately?

# Justice

Masonic ritual teaches that *justice is that standard, or boundary of right, which enables us to render to every man his just due, without distinction. This virtue is not only consistent with Divine and human laws, but is the very cement and support of civil society; and as justice in a great measure, constitutes the real good man, so should it be the invariable practice of every Mason never to deviate from the minutest principles thereof.*

Our brother Freemason Benjamin Franklin said "Justice will not be served until those who are unaffected are as outraged as those who are." We Freemasons must work to bring justice in our world both to places where the need for justice directly impacts us and also to the places where the lack of justice seems to have no impact on us at all. We must do it because we believe in justice for all people at all times.

The most powerful way in which we bring justice to this world is through our personal actions. Freemasons behave justly in all of our conduct and are not afraid to have our actions judged openly. All of our conduct towards others should be without deception. We judge by the facts before us using the best judgement possible without favoritism, prejudice or bias.

# Let Brotherly Love Prevail

Masons are taught to find joy and life-affirming meaning in loving others and in being loved by others. When we gather together in a Lodge we find that we are surrounded by others who share that same value and will offer us their love while accepting ours. Together, Masons pray "Let brotherly love prevail and every moral and social virtue cement us." This community and brotherhood gives us strength to do our work of building a better world through the way we live our lives in a world that may not share that value of brotherly love that we profess.

The work of a Freemason is not only to give and accept love with other Masons but also to share love with the whole world. Masonic ritual in many jurisdictions says *Remember, that every person has a claim upon your good offices.*

St. Francis of Assis understood that truth when he wrote the famous prayer in which he said:

"Lord, make me an instrument of your peace.
Where there is hatred, let me bring love..
Where there is offense, let me bring pardon..
Where there is discord, let me bring union..
Where there is error, let me bring truth..
Where there is doubt, let me bring faith..
Where there is despair, let me bring hope..
Where there is darkness, let me bring your light..
Where there is sadness, let me bring joy..
O Master, let me not seek as much.
to be consoled as to console, to be understood as to understand,.

to be loved as to love,. for it is in giving that
one receives,.
it is in self-forgetting that one finds,.
it is in pardoning that one is pardoned,.
it is in dying that one is raised to eternal life."

As Masons, who have been raised, let us
live lives where brotherly love prevails.

_____

_____

_____

_____

_____

_____

_____

_____

_____

_____

_____

_____

_____

_____

_____

_____

# Let Not Your Zeal

As soon as a man is made a Freemason he is admonished not to let his zeal for Freemasonry lead him into argument with those who may ridicule Freemasonry.

As long as Freemasonry has been around it has had its critics. It likely always will. While it can be tempting to engage these critics in arguments or to attempt to defend our Craft against the negative comments that others may make, we are instead charged to exercise restraint and civil silence instead of engaging in impassioned arguments.

The Christian leader Saint Francis of Assisi is reported to have told his followers "Wherever you go, preach Christ. If necessary use words." He knew that the most powerful witness for his religion was not the words of his followers but their actions and behaviors.

So it is with Freemasonry. We defend our Gentle Craft by living good and moral lives that others respect. This lifestyle will do all that is needed to defend Freemasonry from its enemies and encourage other Good men to seek admission into our order.

# Light, but Partially

On December 12, 1799 our Masonic brother George Washington became ill with a painfully swollen throat. No less than three different physicians were summoned to attend to him and they applied the best medical treatments of their day. These treatments included bleeding him of thirty-two ounces of blood, intentionally blistering his legs and feet in an attempt to "rebalance his fluids," giving him an enema, and having him gargle with vinegar. These treatments did not help and our brother, the first president of the United States died on December 14, 1799.

When we read about the treatments that George Washington underwent in his final days we are shocked and startled by them because today we know much more about the human body and medicine than was known in 1799. No doctor would use these methods to treat a patient with Washington's symptoms today.

In Freemasonry we progress through a series of degrees. In each degree we receive more light than we previously had. This teaches us that in life we are always on a progressive journey of learning and growth.

Humanity is on that journey as a species, with each generation adding to the base of knowledge and building on the work of those who have gone before

The goal of a Freemason is to be better today than he was yesterday, but not as good as he will be tomorrow.

While doing our best now, we must be thankful for those who have gone before us to bring us to the place we are and also hopeful that those who come behind us will advance even farther. This lesson is taught in the Third Degree where we are reminded that *future ages shall find out the right.*

# Mercy

In the Christian Scriptures, Jesus told the following story; "Two men went up into the temple to pray; the one a Pharisee, and the other a publican. The Pharisee stood and prayed thus with himself, God, I thank thee, that I am not as other men *are*, extortioners, unjust, adulterers, or even as this publican. I fast twice in the week, I give tithes of all that I possess. And the publican, standing afar off, would not lift up so much as *his* eyes unto heaven, but smote upon his breast, saying, God be merciful to me a sinner. I tell you, this man went down to his house justified *rather* than the other: for every one that exalteth himself shall be abased; and he that humbleth himself shall be exalted."

The moral of this story is not exclusive to Christianity. It teaches us that a proper prayer between an imperfect man and his perfect God is a humble prayer for mercy.

The story challenges us to be humble. We are always to remember that we are imperfect and in need of mercy from God and others. The story also challenges us to show mercy to others. After all, how can we be harsh to one of our brothers when we ourselves need forgiveness too?

# Otherwise Remained
## at a Perpetual Distance

Every person is born into a set of circumstances that he did not choose and over which he has no control. No man chooses who his parents will be, what country, state or city he will be born in, what generation he will be part of, in what religion (if any) his parents will raise him or what economic circumstances will surround his childhood. These factors that we did not choose help shape each of us into the unique person that we are.

Circumstance will naturally cause us to meet people in similar situations to our own. Our first friends are usually the people who live in the same neighborhood as us, go to the same school or place of worship that we do or play the same sport that we play on the same team that we play on. These opportunities for acquaintance are wonderful. However, they often only allow us to meet people who are not very different from ourselves.

Not so in Freemasonry. Freemasonry is intentionally broad and inclusive in its membership. We discriminate against no man because of his religion, physical appearance, or social status. Freemasonry teaches that it is the internal and not the external qualification that renders a man worthy to be made a Mason. Therefore, in a Masonic Lodge, men of many different backgrounds, experiences and belief systems join together in a union of true brotherly love that transcends the differences that may otherwise separate them in the world.

We do not achieve a form of pretend union by ignoring our differences and pretending that we are all the same even when we are not. Instead, we acknowledge that we may hold different religious, political, and cultural ideas and we still consider each other to be equal brothers even though we are not identical in our thinking. We do not require uniformity to have equal respect and love for one another in Freemasonry.

This special trait of Freemasonry allows men who would otherwise have remained at a perpetual distance to form true friendships together within the fellowship of our Fraternity.

In order to achieve this fellowship, Masonry discourages us from focusing on the things that separate us and encourages us to first focus on the things that we hold in common, such as our love of God, who is our shared Father, and our desire to aid and assist our fellow man. Most of all, Freemasonry encourages us to help each other in our mutually shared goal of personal self-improvement. After all, each of us came to the lodge for the purpose of "improving ourselves in Masonry." By focusing first on the things that we have in common, we will find that we better respect our brothers even when they disagree with us. This connection combats the tendency to dehumanize people with whom we disagree. When we first celebrate and experience our shared humanity and brotherhood, then we can respect the fact that we may disagree about things such as politics or religion while still being much-loved brothers.

# Our Five Senses (Hearing, Seeing, Smelling, Tasting, and Feeling)

Masonic ritual teaches us that God has created humans so that we have five main ways of gathering information. Namely, we can hear, we can see, we can smell, we can taste and we can feel.

Our ritual traditions make use of many of these senses throughout the ceremonies whereby we are initiated as an Entered Apprentice (first degree), passed to the degree of Fellow Craft (second Degree) and raised to the sublime degree of Master Mason (third degree). Our ceremonies teach using these methods because these are the ways that the human being has been designed by God, the

Great Architect of the Universe, to receive and process information.

Remembering this design teaches Freemasons to consider all data and facts when making a decision. It teaches us to avoid pre-judging a situation, but instead to consider each detail and possible piece of evidence before rendering a verdict when we face a choice. We are to make informed decisions, considering every possible thing that we can observe in any way.

This method of decision- making combats prejudice and other biases and encourages us to be honest and just judges who make the best and most informed decisions possible in all matters before us from those which seem trivial all the way to those which are matters of great importance.

*Making Good Men Better*

# My Trust is in God

In his twenty first Psalm, David wrote "Some trust in chariots, and some in horses: but we will remember the name of the Lord our God. They are brought down and fallen: but we are risen, and stand upright."

We Masons, like the shepherd boy David who became King of Israel after his defeat of the giant Goliath against all odds, put our trust in God.

We know that God's power cannot be measured by man. We know God to be the Great Architect of the Universe whose plans are perfect. Yet, we cannot see, during its construction, the full beauty of the world that God is in the process of building.

Like the Operative Masons who labored on the building of Solomon's temple, we see only the part of the work we are currently working on and the work of others who have gone before us or are currently working alongside of us. We as builders, rather than architects, lack the perspective to see how all of our work will eventually fit together and create a thing of beauty and purpose. But, since we trust the Great Architect, we labor according to our instructions even when we cannot personally see the full result yet. We trust in God.

Consider a beautiful tapestry or needlework sampler. From the front side it is a thing of beauty but from the back it is a clog of string going in many different directions and appears to be an example of chaos. When we are in the process of living our lives on this earth, we are building. We are laboring according to the Architect's directions. We are looking at the back side of the tapestry and sometimes what we see makes no sense. Yet, we trust that the Grand Architect's plans will produce a thing of beauty on the front side that only he has the perspective to see at this time..

Our trust is in God. We trust that as we labor faithfully, even though we do not see the total plan at this time, that someday we will hear the words *Well done thou good and faithful servant, enter thou into the joy of thy Lord.*

# Pay The Craft Their Wages,
## If Any Be Due

A specific duty of one of the Lodge's principle officers is to "pay the craft their wages, if any be due." Obviously, in today's speculative Masonic lodges our members do not receive money. However, in ancient times, when Masons were constructing buildings their prompt payment was a matter of great importance.

The Biblical book of <u>Deuteronomy says in chapter 24 verse 15</u> "You shall give him his wages on the same day, before the sun sets (for he is poor and counts on it), lest he cry against you to the Lord, and you be guilty of sin."

Freemasons learn from our ritual to always give people what we owe them when they are owed it. We consider meeting our financial obligations to others to be a moral duty that we are proud to perform.

# Plumb

A tool often explained in the Fellowcraft degree is the Plumb or Plumb Line. It is like a level for vertical things; it tells us if something is perfectly vertical or if it is askew.

The Plumb Line reminds to live a life that is upright, honest and just. Masonic ritual says *As an Insecure building must eventually fall, so he whose life is not supported by an upright course of conduct can no longer sustain a worthy reputation and must soon sink beneath the estimation of every good and virtuous man.*

Other Masonic ritual tells us that the *plumb admonishes us to walk uprightly in our several stations before God and man.*

Like every Masonic working tool, the Plumb contains a lesson that can help us make good choices in each of our daily decisions. Always choose the option that is true and right.

Every choice we make forms the foundation of our life. Build a solid foundation by making decisions and choosing solid options with integrity.

# Pot of Incense

The aroma and smoke of the burning incense rising toward heaven is symbolic of our offering to God. The hotter the fire that burns the incense, the more smoke and smell it will create.

Similarly, the harder we work at living a good life the more pleasing our life will be to God.

This symbol reminds us to never give up in our effort to be the best person we can be. It reminds us that God will be pleased with our work to reach our fullest potential. The harder we work to reach our potential, the more pleasing our life will be in the eyes of our Creator.

Freemasons are workers and we believe our hard work to make ourselves into the best people we can be will help improve the world and thereby please God.

# Prudence

Masonic ritual defines Prudence as our calling to *regulate our lives and actions agreeably to the dictate of reason, and says that Prudence is that habit by which we wisely judge, and prudentially determine, on all things relative to our present, as well as our future happiness.*

When we make prudent decisions we have taken time to thoughtfully consider the implications of our choice, both on ourselves and on others.

Freemasonry calls us to think about our choices and their implications instead of making rash or hot-headed decisions.

Prudence reminds us to reflect upon the moral and social consequences of our activities and our relationship to God.

# Reach of the Cable Tow

Years ago, I was sitting in my office quietly doing paperwork when my secretary burst in screaming that the trash dumpster behind our building was on fire. Without thinking, I jumped from my desk, grabbed the fire extinguisher off the wall outside my door and ran into the alley. I was instantly covered in soot from the burning trash. Flying cinders burned holes in my cotton shirt and singed my silk tie. I emptied the fire extinguisher in a matter of seconds with no discernable impact. At that moment I realized that what I was doing was not helping and I felt a bit foolish for my initial do-it-yourself reaction. I went back inside and sheepishly told my secretary to call the fire department. They came and in a matter of minutes and put out the fire (and recharged our fire extinguisher).

Freemasonry teaches us that we are bound by the limits of our cable tow. Each of us has limits that we cannot exceed. We must know what those limits are, and even while working to improve ourselves and build our skills, we must know what we can and cannot do at any given time and stay within those due bounds.

We are only responsible to perform the tasks that are within the reach of our cable tow, tasks that we are capable of doing well. We must not yield to the temptation of pride and claim that we can do everything alone without help. No man can do everything and there is no shame in asking for, and accepting, help when it is needed.

Also, just as we are limited, we must recognize that every other person in our life has his or her limit as well. We must not ask others to do more than they can do. And, if another person needs our help because he cannot do something that we can, then we are happy to offer our aid as long as it is within the reach of our cable tow.

# Remember your brother's needs in all your applications to deity equal with those of your own

Freemasons believe in God. Each individual Mason is free to understand who God is and how God would be worshipped in his own way according to the dictates of his own conscious. Freemasonry teaches us that we are to pray, yet it leaves the details of how those prayers are to be offered to the personal devotional tradition of each individual brother.

However a Mason prays, be it kneeling in an ornate cathedral, prostrate towards the East, standing with his arms uplifted to the heavens or simply while driving his car down the road, he is instructed to pray for his brothers.

Furthermore, he is instructed not simply to pray for his brothers after he is done praying for himself. No, a Mason is charged to remember the needs of his brothers before God, equally with those of his own. So strong is the bond of Freemasonry upon those who take our craft seriously.

In addition to the spiritual benefits of intercessory prayer, this practice has a great social benefit of increasing the feeling of connection and love between members of the Craft. It also requires us to actually know something about the lives of the men who sit in lodge with us. We must know about their lives, their joys and fears so that we can pray for them in our applications to Deity.

Thus, Masonry puts into practice our true belief in the very real brotherhood of man under the Fatherhood of God.

# Rite of Destitution

At some point in his life, every Master Mason has been in a position where something was demanded of him that he was unable to give.

This important moment teaches us what it feels like to need and not have. Our ritual makes sure that we have that feeling deeply engraved in our being so that we can call upon the power of that feeling in the future to motivate us to positive acts of generosity towards others.

Masonry teaches us to remember that feeling when we see others in life who need something that they do not have. This encourages us to be of a generous and kind spirit when we see others in need. We are not to feel superior to the person in need because we have been there too and we may be there again.

It also reminds us that we all have limitations. We must know what our limitations are and be willing to graciously request and accept help from others when our limits have been exceeded by the demands of life.

# Rough and Perfect Ashlar

In many Masonic Lodges there are two stones or ashlars on display somewhere in the Lodge room. One is in its natural state with jagged and rough edges and the other has been made perfectly square. This is to teach us that *none of us are born into this life fully formed but through intentional effort and with the correct use of moral tools, we can become better than we first were.*

When a man applies the moral teachings of Freemasonry to his life he becomes a better person. He is transformed from the rough and natural state into the state he desires to be in.

Just as the tools of operative Masonry are used to transform the jagged rough edges of a stone from the quarry into a stone with smooth straight edges for use in the construction of a building, so a Freemason can use the moral tools of Freemasonry to transform his life into something that is useful for the benefit of all of society.

# Service

In his inaugural Address on January 20, 1961 United States President John F. Kennedy challenged his fellow Americans with the words, "Ask not what your country can do for you — ask what you can do for your country."

Freemasonry uses the symbol of the Beehive to teach several moral lessons. One of them is *As dependence is one of the strongest bonds of society, mankind was made dependent on each other for protection and security, as they thereby enjoy better opportunities for fulfilling the duties of reciprocal love and friendship. Thus was man formed for a social and active live, the noblest part of the work of God; and he that will so demean himself as not to be endeavoring to add to the common stock of knowledge and understanding, may be deemed a drone in the hive of nature, a useless member of society, and unworthy of our protection as Masons.*

Freemasons are always to seek ways to be of service to others. We are challenged by the teachings of our Craft to be active members of our society, doing all we can to improve the world in which we live.

# Skirrit

The Skirrit is a working tool that is used in some Masonic ritual traditions. It is basically a spool of chalk covered string on a stick. It is similar to the tool that is commonly used today known as a "chalk line." Operative Masons used the Skirrit by driving the stick portion in the ground and then unwinding the chalk covered string in a straight line on the ground so that the string then marked a true straight line on the ground. The operative mason could use this to mark where a foundation or other part of a building may go.

Freemasons use this tool to remind us of the straight and narrow path ahead of us that we should follow. Masonic ritual teaches that *we must ensure that we do not wander from the goal of perfection that we have set.* We must not get distracted from our goal of doing the right thing. Nor can we cut corners or take routes that appear to be shortcuts. Instead we stay true to our course and steadfast in our determination to travel through this life on the moral and upright path in each of our daily decisions and interactions with our fellow men.

In what ways are you tempted to cut a corner or otherwise wander off of the correct path? How do you deal with such temptations in your personal and professional life?

_____

_____

_____

_____

_____

_____

_____

_____

_____

_____

_____

_____

_____

_____

_____

_____

_____

# Spokes on the Wheel

Consider the spokes on a wheel. As the wheel spins a spoke that is on the bottom of the wheel will soon be on the top. Soon it will be back on the bottom again, and then as the wheel continues to turn that same spoke will be back on the top a short time later.

So it is with us as we travel through life. One day we will experience failure and loss. The next day success and gain. Then the day after that we may experience pain and failure again, and the day after that, joy and happiness. So the cycle continues as long as we live.

Reflecting on this reality will teach us never to be devastated by our sorrow because joy will surely follow. It also teaches us never to be arrogant and haughty in our success for a humbling time will soon be upon us. Likewise, when we see another person who is not successful we must never judge them harshly since we do not know what prestige their tomorrow may hold. When we see another person who is highly exalted we must remember that their future may hold different fortunes for them as well.

Therefore, we must treat ourselves and all other people with universal kindness and respect for the intrinsic worth that each human being holds. We must not base our respect for self or others based on failures or accomplishments because both are fleeting.

# Square

A square is one of the most famous working tools of Freemasonry. It is used in the most common symbol of our craft, the Square and Compass. The square is a ruler with a 90- degree angle. In operative masonry, it is used to make clean corners and to help make sure that everything is perfectly lined up when building.

In Freemasonry's Fellowcraft Degree, we are taught that the square is tool is to help *square our actions by the square of virtue* and we are commanded to *act upon the square*; that is, to make our virtues and morals shape every one of our actions.

When we see the square we are to remember that every decision we make should be guided by the goal to be virtuous.

Making virtuous decisions means making choices that are good, righteous, worthy, honorable, moral, upright, and honest. We are to make these choices not just in the big decisions we face throughout our lifetime but also in every small choice we make every day. In fact, it is in making the honorable choice daily in our small decisions that we develop the pattern of making the honorable choice as part of our natural disposition. When this happens, we find that when we are faced with the big and important choices of life that we will naturally bend towards the virtuous option.

In living like this the Mason truly applies this working tool to his life.

# Temperance

Masonic ritual teaches that *temperance is that due restraint upon our affections and passions which renders the body tame and governable, and frees the mind from the allurements of vice. This virtue should be the constant practice of every Mason, as he is thereby taught to avoid excess, or the contracting of any licentious or vicious habit, the indulgence of which might lead him to disclose some of those valuable secrets which he has promised to conceal and never reveal, and which would consequently subject him to the contempt and detestation of all good Masons.*

Temperance means restraint. As Freemasons we strive to control our passions and desires, to practice restraint in all things and to avoid excess. The virtue of temperance reminds us to use thoughtful caution in our actions, words, and interactions with others.

# That He Was Human and Not Divine

In order to be accepted into Freemasonry a candidate must already be a good man. He must also have the desire to become even better. This practice is rooted in the philosophy that no man is perfect. No matter how good we may be, there will always be room for improvement. We remember that only God, the Great Architect of the Universe is truly perfect.

In the Masonic Funeral lecture in some jurisdictions the we say (speaking of the deceased) *Let us cast around his foibles, whatever they may have been, the broad mantle of Masonic Charity. That he had his faults is simply to illustrate that he was human, and not divine.*

Since each of us is imperfect, and if we are honest with ourselves, we are acutely aware of our many flaws, then it holds that we are not in a position of superiority to judge others. Or, in the words of a more modern phrase, people who live in glass houses should not throw stones.

As Masons we are charged with being aware of our own faults and working to improve them. We are also charged to be kind and loving to others who are with us on the journey of life who have their own faults to remedy.

Therefore, let us not judge the faults of others harshly. Instead, let us show grace and forgiveness, casting around their foibles the broad mantle of love.

# The 47th Proposition of Euclid

The 47th proposition or problem of Euclid teaches one of the most important principles of geometry, known to us as the Pythagorean Theorem, which is communicated by the formula $A^2 + B^2 = C^2$ when working with a right triangle where $C$ represents the hypotenuse. We are also taught that whenever a triangle has a side length ratio of three, four, and five, the triangle will be a right triangle.

In many masonic lodges this symbol is used to represent the Past Master of the Lodge. This is appropriate because it refers to working with right triangles which is a reference to the Master's Square. This is to show that the Past Master has learned how to make complex constructions from the simple angle of ninety degrees. This is symbolic of the knowledge and wisdom that a Craft Lodge Past Master has gained from his service to the Craft.

Freemasons believe that through hard work and dedication we can build great things even when we start with a simple foundation.

Also, note the use of the three, four, five length ratio of a right triangle in some jurisdictions. In those ritual traditions, a candidate will traverse the lodge three times as an Entered Apprentice, four times as a Fellowcraft, and five times as a Master Mason, thus "forming a Square" by the time he is raised. This teaches us that perfect work takes time and is a process that cannot be rushed.

The work we do today will lay the foundation for the work that we can do tomorrow. Since our future work is dependent on the quality of our current work, we must always take our time, appreciate the processes of progress and do our best.

# The Common Gavel

The second working tool each Mason is taught to use is called the common gavel. We learn that this tool is used to take a rough stone and make it perfectly even on all sides.

We further learn that vices in our lives cause us to be unbalanced. We are thus encouraged to remove these things from our lives so that we may be useful. After all, they waste our time, money and talents.

Just as a jagged piece of rock cannot be as useful in making a building as a perfectly square piece of rock can be, so we cannot be as useful in society if we are bogged down by addictions or wasteful activities that take our time, money, thoughts and energy away from more useful aims.

Breaking rough corners off of stone with a hammer is hard and slow going work, but it is important and must be done in order to fit a stone for the builder's use. So it is with us. Stopping wasteful behavior is not easy and it does not happen all at once, but the end result is worth the effort. Do not give up, do not get discouraged, keep working on this every day just as the Apprentice Masons of old worked each day at their task and were rewarded for their hard work. You will be rewarded for yours, too.

# The Form of a Lodge

When a man becomes a Freemason he is taught that the Lodge room has been intentionally constructed in a particular shape. He is told that it is as long as from East to West and as wide as from North to South and that it is as tall as the heavens. This is to teach the new brother about the concept of universality.

Masons believe that everything in existence has been created by God and therefore the great expanses of creation are where we are to live and work. This teaches us to value and respect different places and to view people from faraway places as equal to us.

Our Masonic brother Samuel Clemens who wrote under the pen name Mark Twain is supposed to have quipped that "travel is the natural enemy of prejudice." This is why Freemasons are encouraged to travel and work. We wish to benefit from the wisdom of those who have different traditions than we do. We find brothers in all races, religions, political systems and geographic regions where many different languages are spoken.

The universal brotherhood of man under the universal fatherhood of God is one of the first lessons a Freemason learns and it is one we must always strive to remember.

# The Level

The Level is a tool whose use is taught in the Fellowcraft degree in most jurisdictions. Operative masons and others use a level to test the horizontals of an object, to make sure that it is smooth, even, and level. We Freemasons use the level is a reminder that *that we come from the same place, share in the same goal, and will eventually be judged by the same immutable law.*

The level is a symbol of equality among brethren in the Lodge and teaches the intrinsic equality of all people.

One of the universal experiences of all human beings is that we are all traveling on the same level of time. Masonic ritual states;

*And for each and all, time will lead us to that undiscovered country from whose bourne no traveler returns.*

Remember that all people are intrinsically equal because it pleased God, the Grant Architect of the Universe to create us this way, in His image. Every member of your lodge stands equal to all others regardless of his background, wealth, race, religion or any other distinguishing factor. All of us have different paths through life but each end in the same way.

# The Pencil

The pencil is a Working Tool used in some Masonic ritual traditions. Operative masons use it for marking down any number of things.

We Freemasons use this tool to teach us that everything we do, good or bad, is being written down by God, and that on the day when we stand before Him, all of these deeds will be lain before us. It inspires us to leave a good mark in our world by a well lived life. It teaches us to be responsible as some Masonic ritual says that each of us *must give an account of his actions and conduct through his mortal life.*

# The Purpose of a Lodge

Freemasonry is not a social club or a service organization.

Our lodges do not exist for the purpose of philanthropic impact in our communities, nor do they exist so that men may have a place to seek entertainment. Freemasonry is not a faith community. Our lodges do not exist as places where men gather to worship God.

Instead, Freemasonry is a lifestyle. In Lodge, Masons are taught the values of our Craft through their personal experience with the ancient rituals that have been used to teach these same values to good men for hundreds of years. This tradition creates a culture that connects us to each other and to those who have gone before us. It also creates a place where those who are coming after us can join us in this mystic union of moral living.

The real art and craft of Freemasonry is lived out in the daily life of each individual Mason through the way he treats his fellow humans. Freemasonry is lived out in each choice that every Mason makes in how he uses his time, his treasure and his talent.

Freemasonry has the effect of philanthropic impact because each Mason makes charitable choices in his daily living as a result of learning the lesson of charity in his lodge's ritual, then the Mason chooses to apply those lessons in his daily life.

Freemasonry has the effect of creating fellowship between Masons because good men who share the same values will naturally seek each other's company and friendship in their life choices.

Because Freemasonry teaches that every Mason should worship and serve God according to his personal understanding and conviction, it positively impacts the various faith communities to which Masons belong. Each Mason will, encouraged by the teachings of our Craft, become a better members of his own Church, Temple, Mosque or religious community.

The purpose of a Lodge is to make Masons. Memorizing every word of a ritual or having perfect attendance at Lodge functions are not the measures of a good Freemason. Putting the teachings of our craft into practice with each decision he makes every day is the true measure of a Freemason.

# Three Great Duties

Freemasons learn that we have three great duties, first to God, second to our neighbor, and thirdly to ourselves.

Every Freemason believes in God and is free to understand God according to the dictates of his own faith tradition and personal experiences. We all agree that God is the parent of humankind and that all humans are God's children. We therefore have the duty to love God as our Father and to communicate with him through prayer as a son communicates with his loving father.

Because all humans are the children of God, we have a duty to our neighbor. We are told that we should treat other people as we would like to be treated and to be fair in all of our interactions with others.

Because we, like our neighbor, are children of God, we have a duty to respect ourselves and to take care of our bodies and minds by working hard to reach our fullest potential both physically and mentally.

What are things you can do to be faithful to God, your neighbor and yourself this week?

_____

_____

_____

_____

_____

_____

_____

_____

_____

_____

_____

_____

_____

_____

_____

_____

_____

_____

# The Trestle Board

Masonic tradition tells us that in ancient times the architect would place the plans for the day's work on a trestle board and the workmen would then consult that plan before starting their work for the day. Throughout the day they could refer back to the designs upon the trestle board to measure their progress and ensure that their building was following the master's plan.

Today we remember that God is the Great Architect of the Universe and has laid out a plan for his creation to follow. Each individual Freemason is free to understand that plan in his own way and to turn to the sacred scriptures and traditions of his religion and faith for personal guidance.

Freemasonry does not stipulate to what Volume of Sacred Law a brother should turn to for guidance in life, it only teaches that whatever that source may be, it should be consulted and followed with regularity and faithfulness.

As a Christian the Holy Bible is the Volume of Scared Law to which I turn. As an Episcopalian, I hear readings from that book several times every Sunday during the worship service and I have a series of assigned readings from the Bible each day as outlined in the Daily Office of our Book of Common Prayer. It never ceases to amaze me how I can be helped by the practical guidance in each day's readings throughout the normal activities of the day.

What is your Volume of Sacred Law and how do you include its regular study in your own life?

Do members of your lodge use different Volumes of Sacred Law and how do they study them in their lives?

If their practices are different than yours, could you benefit by using some of their methods in your own study practices?

_____

_____

_____

_____

_____

_____

_____

_____

_____

_____

_____

_____

_____

_____

_____

_____

_____

_____

_____

# The Trowel

An operative mason will use a trowel to spread cement between layers of brick. In some jurisdictions, this is taught as the only working tool for a Master Mason. The trowel is used to, *spread the cement of brotherly love; that cement which unites us into one sacred band or society of friends and brothers.*

Around the world many different Masonic rituals are used. Lodges vary in style and form from one another greatly across cultures. Even in the same community, one lodge may require black tie as its dress code while a lodge less than a mile away may welcome men to come in blue jeans and work shirts.

Some lodges own grand buildings that are on par with the great cathedrals of Europe while others meet in simple pole barns with cement pad foundations surrounded by corn fields. Some lodges charge dues that only a small percentage of men can afford to pay and others have dues so low that almost anyone can afford to pay them with ease. Some lodges meet every two weeks and others may meet only a few times per year. This great variety within Freemasonry is one of its greatest strengths. It ensures that a good man can find a lodge that meets his needs and wants. However, the thing that every lodge has in common is the cement of brotherly love which unites all Freemasons together into the same brotherhood. Love is what defines the lifestyle and connection of Freemasonry. The sharing of that love is represented by the Trowel.

# Truth

In the Christian tradition it is said that before his crucifixion, Jesus appeared before <u>Pontius Pilate</u> and told Pilate that he had come to bear witness to the truth. Pilate then asked "What is truth?" People in our world today are asking the same question. It is a question to which we Freemasons have an answer.

Freemasonry teaches that truth is *a primary attribute of God and that it is a fundamental principle that all good men strive to emulate.*

Being true means being authentic and genuine, void of pretense or exaggeration. Being true means being honest, accurate and transparent.

Masonic ritual says that *to be good and true is the first lesson we are taught in Masonry. On this theme we contemplate and by its dictates we endeavor to regulate our conduct. Hence, while influenced by this principle, hypocrisy and deceit are unknown among us and sincerity and plain dealing distinguish us.*

I think a good way to describe Freemasonry when a person asks about it is to say that we are a group where hypocrisy and deceit are unknown among us and sincerity and plain dealing distinguish us. May this always be so.

# Youth. Manhood. Age.

Masonry teaches that we all progress through life in three principle stages, namely our youth, our adulthood, and our old age. We are taught that each period of time is special and that we should behave differently in each period of life

During our youth we should learn as much as we can. We should try new things and take more risks. We should travel and have many different experiences. During this stage of life we are to learn skills that will help us for the rest of our life and we are to discover what we like and what we do not like. We are to learn what our strengths are and what our weaknesses are.

During adulthood we are to maximize our strengths and minimize our weaknesses, having learned what those strengths and weaknesses are during our youth. We are to apply the lessons we learned during our youth to work that makes our world better. We are to guide the youth who are coming behind us while also taking care of those who have gone before us with great respect.

In old age ritual tells us to enjoy the blessings of a youth well spent and an adulthood well lived. We are to give loving, kind, and respectful guidance to those who are younger than us. We should continue to do what we can to improve ourselves and our world while honestly recognizing that age has placed limitations on us and we may not be able to do all of the things that we could when we were younger.

During our lives we may find ourselves in different categories at the same time. For instance, a person in his middle aged years who starts a new job may find that he is functioning in that new job as if he were in the youth stage. Take the lessons Masonry teaches us to apply in our youth and apply them in the new job until you learn it. Be open minded, try new things, listen to those who know more than you do. At the same time, that same brother may be in the old age stage in some of his other activities. Perhaps he is a Past Master of the Lodge, so in that part of his life he must apply the lessons of old age to that part of his life while he is applying the lessons of youth to his work life and the lessons of adulthood to his life overall

In what phase of life are you in now? Are there areas of your life where you are in different phases? What are things you are doing right and what are things about your behavior you could improve to function best in the stage of life you are in?

So Mote It Be.

*Carl W. Davis*

# A Final Lesson: The Broken Column

The broken column reminds us of our impending death. It is unpopular and even off-putting to talk about death in our culture today. This was not always the case. Generations ago, when our Masonic ritual was being formed, and people generally died at younger ages than today, and did so at home surrounded by loved ones instead of in sterile medical facilities surrounded by professional caregiving staff, death was a more accepted and talked about part of life.

In fact, when the majority of people lived on farms, or at least in agricultural settings, their daily lives exposed them to the cycle of life and gave them a much different perspective on all parts of life, including its end, than most of us have today.

Freemasonry is not shy in its treatment of death. Freemasons, though of many different faith traditions, all believe in the immortality of the soul. We are not afraid of the fact that our bodies will die. We do not pretend that this eventuality exists only in some far off theoretical future. Rather, we recognize that it is real and imminent. One Masonic lecture tells us that *while a man thinks himself yet ascending to even greater achievements, the scythe of time will surprisingly end his life and his labors on this earth will suddenly cease.*

Every Master Mason is especially aware of this lesson. We must, like our first Grand Master, live a life that we can be proud of, no matter how or when it ends. Having tried our hardest to do as much good as possible each day, and having lived in a way that made the world better for our presence in it, ultimately our trust is in God, so we are not afraid.

*Well done thou good and faithful servant, enter thou into the joy of thy Lord.*